Editing Textbooks

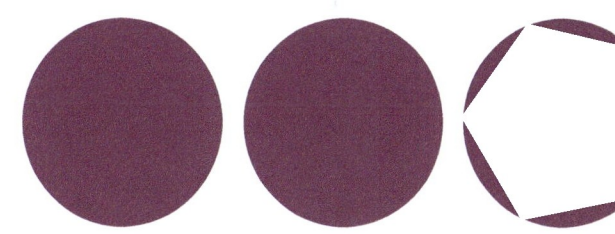

Hetty Marx

First published in the UK in 2023 by
Chartered Institute of Editing and Proofreading
8 Devonshire Square
London
EC2M 4YJ

ciep.uk

Copyright © 2023 Chartered Institute of Editing and Proofreading

ISBN 978 1 915141 16 3 (print)
ISBN 978 1 915141 17 0 (PDF ebook)

All rights reserved. No part of this publication may be reproduced or used in any manner without written permission from the publisher, except for quoting brief passages in a review.

The moral rights of the author have been asserted.

The information in this work is accurate and current at the time of publication to the best of the author's and publisher's knowledge, but it has been written as a short summary or introduction only. Readers are advised to take further steps to ensure the correctness, sufficiency or completeness of this information for their own purposes.

Development editing, copyediting and proofreading by CIEP members
Clare Dobson, Samantha Lacey, and the CIEP's information team.

Typeset in-house
Original design by Ave Design (avedesignstudio.com)
Images from Pexels and Shutterstock

Contents

1 | An introduction to textbook editing   1

    What do we mean by textbooks?   1
    What is different about editing textbooks?   4
    Different kinds of textbook editing   5
    Experience needed for editing textbooks   6
    Reasons for working in this area   8
    How to find work as a textbook editor   9
    The focus of this guide   9

2 | Working with publishers, packagers and authors   10

    Working with publishers and packagers   10
    Working with authors   10
    Workflow   11
    Working practices   15
    Schedules   16
    Budgets   16

3 | The reader   18

    Language level   18
    Content level   19
    Culture, diversity and inclusion   19

4 | Content and structure   24

    Planning content and structure   24
    Checking content and structure   27
    Use of headings   28
    Signposting   29

5 |	The main text	31
	Length	31
	Writing style	32
	Explanations	34
	Legal and ethical aspects	34
6 |	Pedagogical features	35
	Editing pedagogical features	35
	Activities	37
	Boxes	40
	Key terms and glossaries	40
	Start-of-chapter features	41
	End-of-chapter features	42
7 |	Artwork, tables and permissions	44
	Artwork and tables	44
	Permissions	48
8 |	Multi-component products	49
	Editing multi-component products	49
	Related work in educational publishing	51
9 |	Resources	52

like a laptop, tablet or ereader. Others are 'enhanced ebooks', which contain the same material as the printed textbook but add features like interactive activities, video and audio.

Many textbooks are accompanied by a whole host of resources, and a textbook editor will often work on these too. Resources for students include websites with quizzes, flashcards, videos etc and printed resources like workbooks and revision guides. Publishers often provide online resources for teachers to use with their students, such as question banks, PowerPoint slides, lecture notes and figures from the textbook. They may also publish teacher resources with teaching ideas, lesson plans and worksheets.

1 | An introduction to textbook editing

This guide is an introduction to editing textbooks. It is primarily aimed at editors who have some knowledge of the publishing world and of core editing skills, and who are interested in applying this knowledge to editing textbooks and other educational materials.

What do we mean by textbooks?

Broadly speaking, a textbook is a book written for students to help them learn about a subject. Textbooks are likely to be written for:

- a particular subject or topic (for example maths, science, ecology or social theory)
- a certain level (for example 5th year of primary school, 2nd year of undergraduate degree or English language level C1)
- (for school textbooks) a specific curriculum (for example the National Curriculum in England or Scottish Curriculum for Excellence) and/or exam board (for example Edexcel or AQA).

Textbooks are mainly used in:

- primary and secondary schools
- colleges (academic and technical)
- universities
- on-the-job training
- English language teaching (ELT) classrooms.

Traditionally textbooks have been printed books, but now many textbooks are available as both printed books and ebooks. Some ebooks are identical to the printed book, but available to read on a device

Some notes on terminology

A few education-related terms that will come up throughout this guide include curriculum, qualification, exam board and specification. By 'curriculum' we mean the country's national curriculum, which is a set of requirements from the government about what students should learn in each school year. In later school years students study for 'qualifications' (for example, GCSE English, National 5 Maths or BTEC Engineering). These qualifications are set and awarded by 'exam boards' (also known as 'awarding bodies'). The exam boards create 'specifications' (based on the curriculum) which list the exact content that could be examined.

Some exam boards offer 'international qualifications', like International GCSE or A Level, which are taken by students around the world.

In the UK at undergraduate level, most universities determine the content of their courses and set their own exams (although these may be influenced by subject-specific professional societies).

Note that we will use the term 'students' and 'readers' in this guide to refer to any reader using a textbook in their learning. This encompasses other terms like 'pupils', 'schoolchildren' or 'learners'. We use the term 'teachers' broadly to mean educators, whether teachers or teaching assistants at primary or secondary school, people teaching English as an additional language, or lecturers, instructors and professors at university.

In this guide we will often use 'textbook' as a broad term for the educational materials you are working on, whether a traditional (printed or ebook) textbook or accompanying resources like workbooks or online quizzes.

What is different about editing textbooks?

Editing textbooks requires the core editing skills necessary for any field of publishing. But there are some aspects of textbook publishing that require a different set of skills or knowledge. You might be familiar with some of these aspects from other fields (for example complex designs in illustrated non-fiction, or referencing in academic books). The extent to which you need to actively consider these points will vary according to your role, but it's nonetheless helpful to understand them.

- **Learning**: textbooks are designed to help students learn, and this principle should be at the forefront of most decisions in creating a textbook.
- **Accuracy and scholarship**: accuracy of content and general principles of scholarship (for example, objectivity) are important in textbooks.
- **Differentiation**: textbooks need to support the learning of students with different abilities, interests and learning preferences.
- **Complex design**: textbooks are often full-colour and highly illustrated with several design features.
- **Pedagogical features**: textbooks include a range of pedagogical features, such as boxed features and activities, to help students learn.
- **Multiple components**: editing textbooks often involves also editing accompanying material, like worksheets or online quizzes.
- **Multiple stakeholders**: textbooks need to appeal both to the student reader and, usually, to their teacher, who will either purchase the textbook for the class or will require/recommend students purchase it. In some cases, a textbook will also need to be approved by an exam board (if it is asked to endorse the textbook) or by ministry officials in other countries (if the textbook is intended for an international audience).
- **Curriculum and qualifications**: at school level most textbooks are written in line with a national curriculum and, for examined subjects, often in line with a specific exam board's specification.
- **Competition**: your client is likely to have planned the textbook with competitor books (other textbooks for the same course from other publishers) at the forefront of their minds. The main competition's features may influence the publisher's decisions on things like length, coverage, pedagogical features and online resources.
- **New editions**: successful textbooks are likely to be put into new editions, which are sometimes written by new authors.

Different kinds of textbook editing

A number of editing professionals are involved in editing textbooks. The exact nature of each role varies between projects and there is often a lot of crossover in the work expected of each editor. Table 1 provides a very brief overview of some of the roles.

Table 1: A brief overview of publishing roles

Role	What's involved?
Commissioning editor	Develops and manages a list of books, including proposing new books, finding authors and overseeing many aspects of the publishing process. Might have some involvement in editing text (for example, sample chapters). Makes decisions and manages relationships. Traditionally an in-house role but may be freelance.
Project manager/ desk editor/ production lead	Works with the commissioning editor, author(s) and freelance editors to manage the project, from the commissioning stage through to publication. May be split into two roles (before and after completion of the manuscript). Either in-house, packager (see **chapter 2**) or freelance role.
Development (or developmental) editor	Works with the commissioning editor or project manager and author(s) to develop the textbook, usually editing chapters in batches. Considers whether the book works as a whole and whether it maps to the specification appropriately (if applicable). Involves checking the writing style, level, length, structure, features, artwork etc. May involve rewriting text for clarity, length, style and consistency. Either in-house or freelance.
Copyeditor	Edits the complete manuscript. Checks spelling, punctuation and grammar. Applies house style and marks up for typesetting. Checks artwork, tables, references and answer keys. Considers writing style, readability, consistency and accuracy. Liaises with the author(s). Usually freelance.
Fact-checker	Checks the accuracy of the information in the manuscript. Usually freelance.
Proofreader	Checks proofs for spelling, punctuation, grammar and sense. Checks artwork, layout and formatting, and for missing material. Deals with overmatter. Usually freelance.
Indexer	Identifies key terms to be included in the index and specifies page numbers or locators, usually at proof stage. Usually freelance.

While we hope this guide will be useful for anyone involved in publishing textbooks, it is aimed particularly at development editors and copyeditors. As there is a lot of overlap between the two roles and exact briefs vary by project, we use 'editing' to mean development editing and copyediting (and 'editor' to mean professionals in those roles). Unless we specify otherwise the advice will be relevant to both roles (at least on certain projects).

As an example of the overlap between both roles, a development editor may check that the activities in a textbook serve their intended purpose and are at a suitable level throughout the book. Both the development editor and copyeditor will likely check the activities are consistent and clearly worded, and that answers are provided. A copyeditor will tag the activity for typesetting.

When reading the guide, consider your brief and where your role fits in the process. Broadly speaking a development editor has more scope to suggest or make larger changes than a copyeditor (providing there is the time and budget to do so). For example, a development editor might suggest that a particular activity type isn't working well or that all the activities are too difficult and ask the author to revise the activities throughout the book; the copyeditor would then focus on specific activities and ask the author to tweak the wording on some individual questions, for example if there is ambiguity.

Experience needed for editing textbooks

Who can be a textbook editor?

Training and experience in general editing (whether development editing or copyediting) is of course essential. Beyond that, arguably the most important skill is understanding textbooks and education. Just like fiction editing, where editors need to understand characterisation and narrative arc, for textbook editing you need to be familiar with how pedagogical features are used to help students learn and the expectations students and teachers will have about textbooks.

If you don't already have that experience (perhaps from having worked in-house at a textbook publisher or having used textbooks as a teacher),

1 | An introduction to textbook editing

spend time in a bookshop or library picking up textbooks at different levels and in different subjects. Read a chapter or section from each book and see how different writing styles engage and inspire you (or confuse and bore you) and how they vary for different ages and subjects. Look at the pedagogical features and think about which would best help you learn about the subject. The preface will often include a list of these features with explanations of why they are helpful. Look at how various elements are styled differently, like conversations and word lists in an ELT textbook. If you can't visit a bookshop or library in person, use the 'search inside' feature online.

To gain a better understanding of the textbook market it is invaluable to talk to teachers. You can also get a good idea of what teachers are looking for and the issues they face by reading industry blogs and magazines or listening to podcasts.

Do you need subject expertise?

The answer to whether you need subject expertise is ... it depends. Sometimes a client will specify the level of subject knowledge they expect. But if not, you will need to use your own judgement. There are advantages to editing a subject that you haven't studied: it is a lot easier to put yourself in the reader's shoes if you are not an expert. A good rule of thumb is to have the level of expertise that a student might have at the start of the course. So an editor with a social science background might happily edit a first-year undergraduate sociology or law textbook but might hesitate about a third-year textbook that builds on the knowledge acquired in previous years of the degree.

What makes a good textbook editor?

Beyond the experience mentioned earlier in this section, certain attributes will help you succeed as a textbook editor. Perhaps most essential is being thorough and very well organised, to keep track of consistency over multiple features, components and so on. It also helps to have stamina to maintain standards over long projects. Being calm and unflappable (at least on the surface!) in response to inevitable changes, unexpected issues and tight deadlines will also be of great use.

Reasons for working in this area

Editing textbooks can be very rewarding. Education is important and there is great satisfaction in knowing that a clear explanation in a textbook will help students grasp a concept. Like other areas of editing, you can use your creativity to find elegant solutions to problems. Textbooks are complex projects and require good organisational skills, and this combination of organisation and creativity provides variety and satisfaction when it all goes well.

It offers opportunities to learn about new subjects and sometimes to learn new skills (like editing digital products). As textbook projects are often large (with multiple components), textbook editing can be a good source of work.

How to find work as a textbook editor

Cold emailing is often an effective way to find work, although it can take time before you see results. Look on publisher websites or LinkedIn to identify who to contact at a textbook publisher, for example a commissioning editor or member of the production team. Consider starting by approaching editors working on subjects you are familiar with. Emphasise your relevant experience (for example, teaching experience, subject knowledge or experience editing related books). Similarly, consider cold emailing packagers (see **chapter 2**).

The focus of this guide

We focus on textbook editing for UK publishers (note that this doesn't mean exclusively UK readers) and refer to the school and university systems in the UK, but much of the content can be adapted to textbook publishing elsewhere in the world. We do not provide detail on general editing tasks, as other resources and training cover these in detail; instead the focus of the guide is on how to apply your general editing expertise to create textbooks that help students learn.

2 | Working with publishers, packagers and authors

Textbooks are usually published by mainstream publishing houses. While occasionally a university department or an educational charity will publish its own textbook, there isn't the kind of self-publishing market you see in fiction. That means that textbook editors' clients are mainly either publishers, or packagers employed by publishers.

Working with publishers and packagers

For higher profile textbooks you can expect a close working relationship with your in-house contact. They are investing significantly into the success of the book. Textbooks tend to be more closely associated with the publisher than the individual author, so if a textbook is poorly received it can damage the publisher's whole brand. Given this, your in-house contact may be involved in editing sample chapters and discussing features with you, especially during the development editing process.

Textbook publishers sometimes employ a 'packager' (also known as a project management company) to manage the process from manuscript (or sometimes even initial idea) through to the completed textbook. Packagers usually outsource most of the steps involved, including using freelance development editors, copyeditors and proofreaders. The CIEP fact sheet **'Working with Packagers'** provides more details, including some pros and cons of working with packagers.

Working with authors

Textbook authors are usually teachers. They are likely to be experts in the subject and in education. While some are very experienced textbook authors, others might have less writing experience and may need a lot of support. Also they are often working full time in addition to writing, which can be challenging for schedules.

Textbooks are often written by a small group of authors. This can help with the schedule and bring wider expertise to the project, but may introduce inconsistency in style and approach. With the possible exception of edited volumes (those with a different expert author for each chapter) textbooks should be consistent throughout, so editors need to look out for differences and help resolve them.

As with all traditional publishing, authors and publishers sometimes disagree (about content, wording, illustrations etc). You may find yourself in an awkward position of having a close working relationship with the author, but needing to follow your client's (the publisher's) brief. Because publishers are usually very particular about what they want from a textbook, and because new specifications are often subject to last-minute changes, you may find you have to edit the text quite heavily or ask the author for substantial revisions, which requires tact and empathy. While you may be expected to handle most communication with the author, your client should provide support in case of dispute.

Workflow

We will go through an example of how a textbook might go from an initial idea to a printed book, but be aware that publishers differ in their workflows. Importantly, remember that textbooks are complex products so even in the best-case scenario the workflow will rarely be as linear as the following suggests (and in reality it will often be a lot messier).

Commissioning

Imagine that an in-house commissioning editor identifies the need for a new textbook. They draw up a plan for the textbook and find an author to write it. At this very early stage they may ask a development editor to help refine the plan (researching competitor books, developing a pedagogical features plan etc) and to write the detailed author brief. However, the development editor often joins the project once these early points have been decided.

Writing and development editing

The author typically writes a sample chapter and the commissioning editor (and sometimes the development editor) checks the features work as intended and the author is competent at following the brief. The author then writes the rest of the textbook, which the development editor edits and returns to the author to revise. Sometimes the development editor can work on the complete manuscript in one go, but often they'll receive batches of chapters from the author and work on these in stages. Key development editing tasks include:

- checking the author(s) have fulfilled the author brief
- checking the content and structure work and (if relevant) match the specification
- assessing the suitability of the level and style of writing for the intended reader
- ensuring activities and features follow the brief, work as intended and help students learn
- checking artwork and tables for clarity, relevance and suitability for the reader.

As a development editor you might be responsible for project managing the author's delivery of chapters and revised chapters. You might also be the author's main point of contact during development.

Copyediting

The developed manuscript is sent to the copyeditor, who edits it, returns it to the author with queries and then checks the revised manuscript. They submit the copyedited and marked-up manuscript to the in-house team along with various handover forms. Key copyediting tasks include:

- checking spelling, punctuation and grammar, and applying house style
- checking all parts of the textbook are present and in the right order
- tagging the manuscript for typesetting
- checking the manuscript for language level and style
- checking activities work, are presented consistently and have answers (if required)

- checking artwork, tables and references for accuracy and consistency
- dealing with artwork (separating out and numbering the artwork, completing artwork logs and briefs etc).

Typesetting, picture research and proofreading

The manuscript is typeset and artwork is created or sourced. The proofs are checked by the in-house team, a proofreader and the author – and often the development editor and copyeditor. The project manager or proofreader collates the necessary changes from everyone onto one set of proofs. There are usually at least three (and often several more!) rounds of proofs with different people involved at each round.

Other stages

At the same time as the writing and editing, other processes are running. These include development of other components (see **chapter 8**), permissions clearing, sales and marketing, indexing, cover design, blurb writing, text design, peer review and exam board endorsement. As an editor you might be asked for your input into some of these, for example creating a log of copyrighted material that may need to have permissions cleared. In particular, development editors might be involved in checking the text design and facilitating peer review and endorsement.

Text design

The in-house team briefs the designers to create the text design and the designers produce a sample. This sample should show how each of the planned features will be presented, the placement of artwork, all levels of subheadings, the start and end of the chapter, and so on. You may be asked to check that all the required elements are present and to use your knowledge of the content and readers to identify potential issues. The design stage can be quite an involved process, especially if the textbook is heavily illustrated or has many features.

Peer review

The publisher may want to seek feedback from teachers, subject specialists, fact-checkers or sensitivity readers. The peer review process includes finding potential reviewers, asking them to complete a review, sending them chapters, ensuring deadlines are met, collating and summarising their reviews and providing feedback and recommendations to the author.

A development editor may be asked to do some or all of these tasks. The organisational aspects require good project management skills. Turning the reviews into useful feedback for the author goes beyond the scope of this guide but a few pointers include:

- check whether the client wants the author to see the full reviews or only a summary (to avoid them feeling overwhelmed, or to soften blunt wording)
- provide guidance to the author about what feedback they should implement, especially if the feedback is contradictory or the suggestions are not feasible
- be very careful to keep reviews anonymous if this is important.

Endorsed textbooks

If the textbook is designed for a particular qualification, such as iGCSE Chemistry or A Level Philosophy, the publisher may apply to have it endorsed by the exam board. In that case, the development editor and copyeditor will need to be aware of any extra requirements or restrictions from the exam board, for example how examinations can be discussed in the textbook.

You may be asked to complete submission forms, including mapping the manuscript content to the specification and confirming that any other requirements have been followed (or providing an explanation if not).

Check these forms at the start of the project and keep detailed notes as you go along to make the process easier.

The specification is often published shortly before the textbook needs to be published. This means textbooks are often written based on a draft specification, which can result in last-minute changes to the textbook in response to changes to the specification. In addition, during the endorsement process the exam board might suggest or require changes, which result in changes to the text being made during copyediting or even at proof stage.

Working practices

At the start of a textbook project you may receive a large number of files from your client with background information about the specification, the rationale for the project, the market, pedagogical features, artwork briefs and so on. This can be overwhelming, so set aside some time to familiarise yourself with the essential information and make notes about where to find other information as and when you need it during the project.

Usually textbook editors work on the text in Word files and edit using a combination of silent and tracked changes plus comments. For some projects you might revise sentences or paragraphs directly. For example, a school textbook in a series might have a very uniform style and a strict word count to fit a topic per page, so you will make changes directly. For other projects (for example a university textbook by a well-known expert) it may be more important that the author's style is maintained and it would be more sensitive to suggest changes in comments, leaving it to the author's discretion whether to make the amendments.

Tagging (coding/marking-up) the manuscript is a significant part of copyediting textbooks. It may involve adding tags in much the same way as in other areas of publishing (but likely on a bigger scale). For example, indicating A heads using <A> or key terms boxes using <key term>. Some publishers have complex design specifications that you need to follow. Other publishers use specific templates and plugins to mark up text for formatting; in this case be aware that it will involve more set-up time the first time you work with the publisher.

As with most editing projects, there are likely to be conflicting priorities (for example between quality, the schedule, the budget and the author's limited time); this means it may be difficult to solve every issue in a manuscript. If in doubt, check with your in-house contact about what to prioritise. Similarly, when you receive the author's revised chapters there may be a few queries that they haven't answered or actioned. That might be because they disagree with your comment, they need more advice or they simply missed that query. Their revisions might also raise new queries. Keep in mind that time for further revisions is likely to be tight (and you might also start to test your author's patience) and prioritise the more essential changes in any further rounds of revisions.

Schedules

Keeping to schedule is essential. If a textbook is not published before the course starts, teachers may not use it and a year's worth of sales can be lost. If another publisher's textbook comes out in time and is chosen instead, several years of sales can be lost as teachers prepare course materials for a specific textbook and are often reluctant to switch to another.

But textbooks are complex and with complexity comes potential for delay. Authors may struggle to fit writing in around their day job. Reviews often arrive late. Publishers often set optimistic schedules. Expect and be prepared for delays when working on textbooks. If you can help the publisher by fitting in the work despite the delay or by finding solutions (perhaps working on batches, even if this is not ideal), they will be grateful.

Schedules are often long, which can be an advantage in terms of continuity of work, but can be tricky if you are trying to balance more than one project at a time.

Budgets

Development editors are usually contracted before the manuscript has been written. This means that when you agree a budget with your client you are unlikely to know the quality of the writing, the exact word count, the number of artworks and tables, or how adept the authors will be at revising their chapters (will you need to check one, two or more rounds of revisions?). You might not even know how many authors will be involved, and indeed whether there will be a change in the author team part way through.

Given these uncertainties, rather than agreeing a fixed fee it may be sensible to quote based on an hourly rate (although clients will probably want to agree a maximum fee). Throughout the project keep checking that you are on track to complete the work within the agreed maximum fee and raise any concerns as soon as possible. It helps to be clear about any assumptions you've made when agreeing the maximum fee, so that you can explain the need for more budget (for example a longer manuscript, more authors, more rounds of revisions).

Copyeditors are more likely to be offered a fixed fee, and will need to assess whether it is suitable. Remember to think about the complexity and unpredictability of textbook projects and also to allow time for checking any additional components if required. If you are new to working on textbooks try not to underestimate how time-consuming tasks like tagging a feature-heavy manuscript or working with artworks (checking them, pulling together artwork briefs, creating an artwork log etc) will be.

For all editors, keeping detailed records of time spent on projects will help with quoting for future projects. The CIEP guide '**Pricing a Project**' provides useful advice.

3 | The reader

The reader should be at the forefront of your mind when editing textbooks. How old are they? What prior knowledge of the topic do they have? What is their cultural background?

Language level

The language used in a textbook needs to be at the right level for the intended reader. Students should be challenged by the topic, but not impeded by difficult vocabulary and syntax. At the other extreme, using vocabulary that is too simple can patronise students and prevent a full exploration of the topic.

Some topic-related vocabulary will be new to students and may be difficult to understand. Ensure new terms are explained when they are introduced and/or defined in the glossary or key terms boxes (if these features are included in the book – see **chapter 6**).

Most words in the textbook will not be topic specific. For these you need to check the level is appropriate for the reader's language ability. Consider the age of the reader and also whether the textbook is aimed at a subset of the year group, for example by their predicted level of achievement. Also consider whether most readers will have English as a main language or as an additional language (for example textbooks for ELT courses, International A Levels, or for some undergraduate courses).

Younger readers might need simpler vocabulary and shorter sentences and paragraphs. For those with English as an additional language who are less confident reading in English:

- choose plain vocabulary over unusual or pretentious words
- keep sentences to a manageable length (particularly avoiding too many subclauses)

- keep paragraphs to a manageable length
- ensure it is clear what pronouns refer to (and keep them to a minimum to avoid confusion)
- use more active than passive constructions
- avoid idioms and colloquial language.

Many of these suggestions may also be helpful for textbook readers more generally. But note these are very broad generalisations and editorial judgement is important when assessing the suitability of language.

Content level

What prior knowledge of the subject can you expect the reader to have? For school textbooks up to around the age of 16 you can assume that most students will have covered the curriculum up to that age. But beyond that it can be more difficult to be sure what background knowledge a student will have. Someone taking a first-year undergraduate economics module may have recently studied economics and maths at school so will be familiar with many economics terms and confident tackling the more mathematical aspects of the course. However, many students will never have studied economics and school maths might be a fading memory.

Check that any assumed knowledge is reasonable. Encourage authors to add brief recaps if needed. But long explanations of concepts that most readers should be familiar with from previous study could be cut or reduced.

Culture, diversity and inclusion

The area of culture, diversity and inclusion is too broad and fast moving to provide a thorough overview here. The content in this section is only a starting point. There are areas and issues to consider that aren't mentioned here; editors should be aware of equality, inclusion and diversity principles, and that approaches, terminology and guidance will change over time. Also see **chapter 9** for some suggestions of websites for further details.

Inclusion

Where possible there should be a broad coverage of people with different identities (including gender, sexuality, age, ethnicity, socioeconomic status and disability). Ensure fictional names represent different genders and cultural backgrounds.

However, be alert to people only being included because of their identity (for example ethnicity or disability); this is known as 'tokenism'.

Photos and illustrations should include a broad range of identities. Watch out for photos or illustrations of body parts (such as hands on a musical instrument or anatomical drawings) to make sure they aren't all the same ethnicity. Remember that the same checks also apply to cartoons and line drawings.

More broadly, remember that the students using the textbook vary in many ways, such as their identities, interests, abilities, learning preferences and so on. Variety can be a useful tool to help each student feel the textbook is relevant to them and that it helps them learn. For example, a range of examples, extracts (from publications) or vignettes will increase the chance that students will find some that feel relevant to them. A variety of activity types and ways of presenting information will mean students with different learning preferences are supported.

Stereotyping

If certain groups are presented in a stereotypical way, in particular due to their gender, sexuality, age, ethnicity, socioeconomic status or disability, you may want to discuss possible changes with the publisher. For example, are women depicted as caring, weak and emotional? Do men hold high-status jobs while women have lower-status jobs? Are people in different socioeconomic groups depicted differently in terms of their interests and abilities?

Pay careful attention to photos, where stock images can perpetuate stereotypes or, alternatively, can look like tokenism.

Note that, with the exception of any offensive stereotypes, the aim is to present a balance. Taking the earlier example, photos of men in high-status jobs among other photos of women in similar roles is not a problem.

A similar issue is making generalised statements about a particular group. Where this is necessary, make sure it is non-judgemental, avoid oversimplifications, consider using qualifiers (like 'many' or 'some') to avoid suggesting uniformity and (if appropriate) support with evidence.

Language

Preferences for language use for different identities change over time and there is often debate about the most acceptable language to use. If you are unsure it is best to flag any potentially problematic terms to your in-house contact. There are useful resources in **chapter 9**.

Cultural considerations

If you are working on a textbook aimed at an international market (for example for the ELT market or for an International A Level curriculum), it is important to consider different cultural sensitivities and what readers in the target markets may find inappropriate. In addition, in some countries teachers can only use government-approved textbooks, so the publisher will risk losing sales if certain material is included. Ask your client for a list of issues to look out for. Some common ones include avoiding mentioning (or doing so carefully and considerately) sex, alcohol, smoking, recreational drugs, gambling, swearing, certain animals (such as pigs and dogs), certain food (particularly certain animals as food), religion and geo-politics.

Check photos and illustrations carefully for bare skin, alcohol, drugs, weapons and certain animals. Watch out for hand gestures, which can have different (and sometimes offensive) meanings in some cultures. Remember to check all parts of the photo rather than just the main subject. Check maps carefully for sensitivities about borders, country names and flags.

Note that sometimes the specification requires coverage of some of these points (for example gambling disorders in psychology or reproduction in science), in which case check the coverage is sensitive and respectful and avoid unnecessary photos. You could flag the material to your in-house contact along with a note that coverage is required by the specification.

Age

Ensure content, examples and photos are appropriate for the age of the reader. What is acceptable will vary by age and context but tread carefully with any coverage of sex, alcohol, smoking and upsetting material (things like violence, war and death).

Also check examples are suitable and relevant to the reader's age. If you provide an example of spending money, you might pick spending pocket money on toys in a book aimed at eight-year-olds but paying for rent or buying textbooks in a book aimed at university students.

Geographical location

Consider where the readers live. School textbooks are usually aimed at a particular national curriculum, but some are published for an international curriculum. University and ELT textbooks are often aimed more broadly. For any textbook aimed at a range of countries avoid bias towards a particular country (for example providing only UK statistics or referring to 'the government' rather than specifying 'the UK government').

Make sure examples chosen are relevant. Successful US undergraduate textbooks are often adapted for the UK market and that might include changing examples of sports, food, national celebrations, animals or plants to those more familiar in the UK.

Accessibility

In textbook publishing, 'accessibility' often refers to ensuring the text is written at a level that is suitable for the age of the reader. In this subsection we are thinking about 'accessibility' in the sense of not excluding readers due to disability.

Editors have limited scope to improve accessibility (most decisions are made by production or online teams) but we can help in a few ways:

- For ebooks or online material encourage alt-text (a written description of an image, which can be read aloud by screen readers) for images and subtitles for video/audio.
- Where colour is used in figures, make sure the colours are easily distinguishable and avoid referring to elements of the figure by colour alone.
- Consider the legibility of the colours chosen for the text and background (and the combination of the two).
- Encourage use of headings and subheadings.
- Use descriptive text in links ('view the latest data' rather than simply 'click here').

4 | Content and structure

The principles behind planning the content and structure of a textbook are similar in some ways to other types of non-fiction books. For example, textbooks should be divided into chapters, which are in turn divided into sections and subsections. They should be structured in a logical and helpful way, whether that is by topic or chronologically. Where textbooks differ is that they are often heavily influenced by a curriculum or specification.

Planning content and structure

Decisions about content and structure have often been made before a textbook editor joins a project, but your feedback can still be important. There are different considerations depending on the type of textbook, particularly whether or not it is written for a qualification or a curriculum.

Textbooks for qualifications

The content of textbooks that are written for a particular qualification will be largely determined by that qualification's specification, which usually sets out the required content in detail. The author or publisher may have some scope to decide on examples or case studies but the broad content is fixed. Sometimes they may choose to include extension material (that goes beyond the specification) but this may need to be labelled as such in the textbook.

The textbook's structure is also likely to be influenced by the specification, and there might be a close match between the two. For example, if the specification is structured by sections, subsections and bullet points, then the section names may become chapter titles, the subsections become section headings and the bullet points become subsection headings.

There is often some scope to vary the structure a little. For example, if one section has many more subsections than the others, you could consider grouping some together. Or if one of the bullet points is repeated in each of the subsections (perhaps something about research methods) you might pull those together into a new subsection to avoid repetition or to allow greater depth. Just make sure that it is (a) allowed (for endorsed books) and (b) still very clear how the content matches the specification.

If the publisher is aware that teachers often do not follow the order of the specification when teaching, they might decide to either reorder the content, or to keep to the specification order but include more cross-referencing or redefine important terms and concepts.

Textbooks for courses on the curriculum

In the years before students take qualifications (for example GCSEs), their learning is determined by the national curriculum, rather than by an exam board. The curriculum shapes what is taught in schools and teachers may need to follow it to comply with the law. As such, publishers will usually ensure that textbooks cover all the topics in the curriculum. The curriculum may be less detailed than a qualification specification, and so allow some variation (for example the school may be able to choose which country to study in geography).

Ideally textbooks should be structured in the same order as the material is taught in the classroom; this is easier for teachers and means both the authors and teachers can build on knowledge gained earlier in the course.

Textbooks for other courses

For other courses, especially undergraduate ones, there is more freedom for the author to choose the content and structure.

The client or author is likely to have researched the typical content of the course. At undergraduate level it is common for different universities to have some variation in the topics covered on a particular course. The client or author will need to balance providing enough coverage for different universities while keeping the textbook length manageable.

Similarly the client or author will have researched the typical structure of the course. Sometimes there are logical reasons for a particular

structure, like when you need to understand some concepts before tackling others, or a chronological order in history or literature. In other courses there will be a conventional order for the topics (sometimes based on the order of a particularly popular textbook).

Where there are significant differences in the likely order in which a subject is taught, the publisher needs to decide whether chapters should be truly standalone. This is rarely the preferred option as it leads to repetition (if you have to explain concepts again) and can feel disjointed. Alternatively the book could be written on the assumption it will be read in chapter order, but might include additional cross-referencing to help readers who are studying the topic in a different order.

Checking content and structure

You may be asked to check whether the content and structure of the draft manuscript matches that in the book proposal, the curriculum details and/or the qualification specification. Depending on the project and your role (this is more common during development editing than copyediting), you may also need to check content and structure for sense.

For content, consider questions like:

- Does the content feel balanced, or are some topics covered in a lot more detail than others (without good reason)?
- Does anything seem to be missing, like a step in an argument, an evaluation of a theory or an explanation of basic principles needed to understand the content?
- Is the content objective and accurate?
- Has enough content been given to answer activities and exam questions adequately?
- If there is a strict word limit for each topic, has this been adhered to?

For structure, consider questions like:

- Does the discussion flow well through each chapter and through the book?
- Is there a logical progression?
- Does the structure help students understand the topic and remember the key details?
- Are there any topics that would be better moved to earlier in the chapter or book, so students can understand later topics?
- Is there a subtopic that is briefly mentioned various times, that would benefit from having a dedicated section so it can be considered in greater depth?
- Is it clear how the topics and subtopics within a chapter link together?

As an editor you could suggest a revised structure or recommend adding more headings and subheadings; or you could help the author to improve the signposting in the chapter (discussed in the '**Signposting**' section below). You could suggest the author adds or removes content. The course of action you take will depend on aspects of the project (for example whether it is written for a curriculum or needs to align with other resources), the stage of development (larger changes can be made during development editing than during copyediting), the schedule and budget (whether there is time for the author to make substantial changes, and time and budget for you to check those changes), and the author–publisher relationship (whether the author is willing to make larger changes).

Use of headings

Headings are an important tool for guiding a reader through a textbook.

Heading levels

Chapters are divided into sections and subsections, each of which starts with a heading. The headings for the main sections in a chapter are usually referred to as 'A heads', the headings for the subsections within those main sections as 'B heads', and so on through 'C heads', 'D heads' etc (or alternatively 'level 1', 'level 2' etc). In some textbooks these headings will be numbered, for example Section 3.4.2 refers to the second subsection in the fourth section of the third chapter. This is useful if there will be a lot of cross-referencing. General editing principles apply to checking heading levels, including:

- Avoid using too many levels. Three will usually be sufficient, but sometimes four will be appropriate.
- Check whether your client has any requirements about the number of levels and whether the headings are numbered. If you see the text design make sure it includes a design for each level used.
- Consider whether an appropriate number of headings has been used (too many can result in a disjointed narrative; too few could mean long sections of uninterrupted text and a difficulty in following the argument).
- Check there is a logical progression through the heading levels. Each C head should be nested within a B head, which in turn should be nested within an A head. The text shouldn't jump from an A head to a C head. The navigation panel in Word can be really helpful to get an overview of the heading levels in a chapter (if Styles have been applied).

- Check your client's preferences about 'stacked headings' (a heading directly followed by another without any text between). Some publishers are happy with stacked headings but others prefer to avoid them. In that case suggest the author adds a sentence or two introducing the section or subsection between the headings (like the one between the A head 'Use of headings' and B head 'Heading levels' above).

Wording of headings

The publisher may request that headings match wording in the specification, but if you are able to edit the headings then aim to make them clear and unambiguous. If you glance at a detailed table of contents (one with the chapter names and A heads), you should find it easy to infer the contents of each chapter. Ideally they will also be concise. Normally the style will be straightforwardly descriptive (for example 'Equations' or 'The Lorenz curve') but some textbooks format headings as questions ('What did the Romans eat?') or use humour. Check that the headings are reasonably consistent in style and length.

Also ensure the wording of headings matches the content in that section as it's not unknown for changes during the writing process to lead to a mismatch.

Signposting

Signposting refers to techniques used to guide the reader through a chapter (and book). It is reassuring for the reader to know what they will be learning, to understand how what they are reading fits into the topic, and to make links between different parts of the course. Here are some typical ways that textbooks use signposting; if these are not included and you feel they would be helpful, check with the author or client.

- Use introductions to briefly set out what will be covered (at a book, chapter and possibly section level).
- Use short conclusions (again at book, chapter and/or section level) to remind readers what they have learned and to situate it in the context of the chapter or book.
- Use cross-references to link back to what has been covered earlier ('Similar to the concept of X in chapter 3, Y is … ') or to what is coming later ('We will explore this topic in more detail in the section on X.').

- Where appropriate, explain how the content in one section relates to the content in the next section. ('The main issue with this theory is X. In the next section we will turn to a theory developed to address X.')

Do keep in mind, though, that if signposting is overdone then it can feel over the top and formulaic, and can take up a sizeable chunk of the word count.

5 | The main text

Editing the main textual content of a textbook is similar to other projects in many respects. Some important differences are pedagogical features (see **chapter 6**), plus some additional considerations in the areas of length, writing style, explanations and legal/ethical aspects.

Length

As with many publishing projects, keeping to the planned extent is important for textbooks. For some textbooks it is essential that every section of every chapter is a specific length, for example where you need to fit one topic per page.

Even for projects where there is more flexibility on a page-by-page basis, you will still need to keep a close eye on the word count. Exceeding the word limit could mean that the production costs will rise, the publisher may need to put the price up and potential readers may be put off by the length. It may also be a flag that coverage is too detailed or the writing style is too wordy.

While it seems to happen less often, going under the word limit can be as much of a problem as going over. It can mean the book will look insubstantial compared to the competitor books or it may require the publisher to set a lower price. Importantly it may be a flag that not enough detail has been provided.

Flag any length issues with your client early on. In some cases they may be happy to adjust the planned extent, but this should lead to a conversation about the impact on your fee.

You may be tasked with reducing the length (or providing tips for the author to do so themselves). Note that reducing the length strays into deeper levels of both copyediting and development editing, and can be very time-consuming, so make sure your fee is adjusted accordingly. Some general tips are:

- Consider whether any big cuts can be made, including whole chapters, sections or subsections (this is likely to be a decision for the client and author).
- Look out for repetition and cut/reduce where possible (while keeping in mind that repetition can be a useful learning tool).
- If the text is particularly wordy, a more hands-on line edit can tighten up the text and reduce the word count.
- Some methods to reduce the extent (rather than the word count) conflict with creating a reader-friendly text but can be considered if necessary; for example, using fewer (or smaller) images, reducing the font size, and replacing bullets with running text.

Writing style

Writing style includes aspects like whether the writing is formal or informal, uses first or third person, uses longer or shorter sentences and paragraphs, uses personal anecdotes or not, is jokey or serious, prefers passive or active constructions and so on. None of these styles are intrinsically better than others, but as an editor you need to consider whether the choices made:

- are reasonably consistent throughout the book: while there is often room for some elegant variation, some inconsistencies will jar more than others
- are suitable for the intended reader: an overly formal style would be tricky for younger readers; passive constructions can be difficult for readers with English as an additional language
- meet the expectations of the market: this is perhaps more the client's role, but you may be able to offer advice if the style seems wrong for the market, for example a jokey book might be more suitable for a revision guide than a set textbook and some undergraduate subjects have more of an expectation of formal, third-person styles than others
- meet the brief or follow the style of other books in the series (if relevant).

5 | The main text

A copyeditor faced with a complete manuscript would be unlikely to make sweeping changes to writing style. If budget allows, you might offer some rewordings to reduce sentence length or change constructions from passive to active, or flag a joke that seems out of place in an otherwise formal book. However, if you notice the style is wildly different from the author brief or there are significant inconsistencies, do query it with your client as soon as possible.

The development editing stage is a better time to revise the writing style, with changes either made by the author during revisions or by the development editor (if the brief and budget allows).

Inconsistencies in style can be a particular issue in multi-authored textbooks. Authors often have a preferred style, so a single-authored book is likely to be broadly consistent in terms of style, with perhaps small inconsistencies that should be easier to fix. However, even with the clearest of briefs (and writing style is not always clearly identified in the author brief) in multi-authored textbooks individual style will often show through. Sometimes this is fine, particularly at undergraduate level. But if it is a problem, consider what will have the most impact given the time and budget and discuss possible approaches with your client. Some techniques include:

- identify and resolve the inconsistency that feels most jarring
- identify and resolve the inconsistency that takes the least time

- focus on improving the consistency of the more noticeable aspects of the chapter, like chapter introductions, subheadings, boxed features and activities.

Writing style is personal, so discuss your plans with the client and, if appropriate, the author. School textbooks often need to follow a series style very closely, so the author should expect editor intervention. But for standalone textbooks authors may be more protective of their writing style, in which case sensitively worded comments and suggestions may be better than directly amending the text. Your client should advise on the best approach.

Explanations

Another essential aspect of textbook editing is checking that the author has explained the subject clearly. Consider the following questions:

- Can you understand the arguments presented in the text?
- Does the account feel balanced and objective? For example, does it cover both sides of a debate (where this is important) and use a neutral tone to discuss controversies? Does the author avoid presenting their personal views? (This is a complex area, so may involve discussions with your client.)
- Are there any moments that make you think 'but what about ... ?' (there might not be space for all the 'but what abouts' but it may help to acknowledge these points to keep the reader's trust).
- Are there any inconsistencies or contradictions in the explanations provided in different parts of the book?
- Does anything seem to be a mistake? While a full fact-check is not usually included, it's definitely worth querying (politely) anything that appears to be incorrect.

Legal and ethical aspects

As with any type of book, flag any concerns you have about legal or ethical issues like libel, copyright infringement or plagiarism. Query sensitively as you may be mistaken. Consider running your concerns past your client first in case they would prefer to approach the author themselves.

6 | Pedagogical features

Pedagogical features are an essential part of textbooks and one of the main differences from other non-fiction books. Textbook publishers use the term 'pedagogical features' to refer to features in a textbook that help students learn. They include chapter introductions, boxes, activities, case studies, glossaries and conclusions.

Editing pedagogical features

Your role in editing the pedagogical features will depend on whether you are development editing or copyediting, and on how much intervention the schedule and budget allows. A development editor can often ask the author to entirely rewrite certain features, remove some or add more of them, while a copyeditor may be limited to suggesting tweaks to individual features. Keeping your role in mind, you may need to check the following aspects.

Useful learning opportunities

Features clearly need to help students learn. They might do that by allowing students to check their understanding, or broaden their perspective, or apply what they've learned to a different topic, or by enthusing students about the field. Keep this in mind when editing pedagogical features and encourage authors to revise features to make the most of the learning opportunity. For example, the author could add targeted questions to encourage students to actively engage with a case study, rather than simply passively reading it.

Relevance

Features should be relevant to the rest of the chapter. For example, learning objectives should match the content of the chapter, case studies should be clearly connected to the topic, activities should test the topics covered in the chapter, and key terms boxes should explain the most important terms explored in the chapter.

Consistency in purpose and style

Check the pedagogical features meet the author brief in terms of the purpose and style of each feature. Does the feature achieve what the publisher intended it to? Is it written in the style required (for example bullet points versus paragraphs for chapter conclusions)?

Is the purpose and style of each feature consistent between chapters? This is particularly important. It is often an issue with multi-authored textbooks where each author will, quite reasonably, interpret the brief in different ways. In that case check whether your client has a preference between the interpretations (and offer your expert opinion).

Amend the features or work with the authors to bring the features in line with the brief and with the other chapters.

Consistency in frequency and length

Check the features meet the brief in terms of how many of each feature are provided per chapter and the word count for each. Some projects will require high levels of consistency, especially where the text design is very precise. For other projects, especially undergraduate textbooks, the text design may be less prescriptive. For example, it might be acceptable if the length of chapter introductions ranges from 300 to 400 words or if there are between six and nine activities per chapter. Ranges like these will allow a good balance between tailoring the features to each chapter while still ensuring the text *feels* consistent. Ideally any differences between the chapters will be purposeful (for example a broader topic requiring more activities than a narrower one) rather than accidental (such as a more verbose author writing longer introductions than their more succinct co-author). But as always, time, money and tact (author relations) will impact on how much input you will have.

A features tracker spreadsheet is invaluable for keeping track of the number and length of the features. An example is provided in Table 2. You can see that some chapters do not meet the brief. Chapter 3 has an introduction that is too long, has too many debate boxes (some of which are too long) and has too many questions. Chapter 1 doesn't have enough questions. All the chapters meet the brief in terms of number

Table 2: Extract from a features tracker spreadsheet (note a real tracker would have several more columns and rows)

Chapter	Learning objectives *Number of bullets*	Chapter intro *Number of words*	Debate boxes *Number of boxes (words per box)*	Questions *Number of questions*
Brief	5–7 bullets per chapter	250–300 words	2–3 boxes per chapter (150–200 words per box)	10 per chapter
1	5	255	3 (123, 212, 151)	8
2	5	270	2 (140, 135)	10
3	7	350	4 (234, 252, 170, 188)	15
4	5	280	3 (155, 170, 160)	10

of learning objectives, but only one chapter has seven bullets – consider whether this will look inconsistent.

Activities

Activities are a really important feature in textbooks (and online resources). They encompass a wide range of features, including:

- open-answer questions, such as short-answer questions, essay questions, discussion questions, drawing tasks
- closed-answer questions, such as multiple-choice questions (MCQs), matching questions, labelling questions, fill the gaps, ordering activities
- classroom or homework activities, such as create a poster, write a fact file, prepare for a debate, conduct an experiment.

Editing activities

Activities require careful editing, including checking the following points.

Content
- Make sure activities include different levels and test different skills. For some textbooks it will be important to follow a progression of increasing cognitive demand, for example from knowledge, to comprehension, to application, to evaluation (these ideas are based on Bloom's Taxonomy; see **chapter 9** for further reading).
- Check that questions are answerable (or classroom activities are achievable) using the material in the book.
- Make sure each activity tests what it is intended to test.

Format
- Where options are provided (for example for matching, labelling or fill-the-gap questions) ensure each option is only correct in one location and that each location has a correct option.
- For MCQs, check the number of options (usually this should be consistent) and the number of correct options (there should always be at least one correct option; clients may want exactly one correct option per MCQ or may be happy to include more).
- Make sure there is a sensible amount of space (enough but not too much) if students are expected to write in their answers, for example in a workbook.

Wording
- Ensure the wording of instructions, questions and options is unambiguous and encourage clear, concise and plain language where possible. Check for consistency in wording of each type of question or activity.
- Avoid using negatives in questions as this can cause confusion (but if it is necessary, consider having 'NOT' in capitals or bold).
- Check the question wording doesn't give away the answer.
- For MCQs, make sure the distractors (the incorrect options) are neither too close to the correct answer nor totally implausible.
- Check whether there is an agreed list of command words (for example discuss, analyse, evaluate), especially for examined subjects. If there

is, ensure these are used as required by the exam board and/or publisher, for example a question using 'explain' might require a more detailed response than one using 'outline'.
- Exam-style questions (or 'practice exam questions') should be as similar as possible to what students will encounter in the exam. Check the following match the specimen papers:
  » type of questions (short-answer/MCQ/essay)
  » the number of each type and how they are ordered
  » distribution of knowledge/application/evaluation questions (or similar)
  » the mark allocation
  » the command words
  » the use of items or sources if relevant.

Editing answers

If you are asked to check the answers, make sure you factor this in when you assess the fee offered as it can significantly add to the word count (especially if the answers are not included in the textbook extent because they are in a teacher resource or online). Check the following:

- The answers are accurate (if required). Before taking on a project find out whether you are expected to check the accuracy of the answers, and whether you need specialised knowledge if so. Even if this is not part of your brief, do flag anything that appears to be a mistake (especially for MCQs where it's easy to revise the question and forget to revise the options).
- All questions (and all parts of each question) have answers provided.
- The answers are consistent with the text (there are no obvious conflicts with the facts or theories discussed in the text).
- The answers are presented in a way that allows the reader to clearly match the question to the answer. But if possible do this in an economical way (for example use of numbers or brief descriptions rather than repeating the question text).
- The presentation is consistent, for example for essay questions provide either a list of the main points the student should include or fully written answers.
- If a mark allocation is used, the marks match those in the questions.
- If the answers are presented as a 'sample student' response, make sure they read like something a student would write.

Boxes

Some examples of boxed features include:

- Controversy and debates: looking at two sides of a debate or evaluating pros and cons.
- Real-life examples, case studies and source material: bringing the topic to life with extended examples (real or fictional).
- Connections and wider context: relating the learning to other topics in that field or related fields.
- In depth: looking at a historical event, a research study, a country etc in greater detail.
- Reflection: encouraging students to develop their own ideas.
- Research methods and subject skills: encouraging students to 'think like a psychologist' (or scientist/historian etc) and to understand techniques and methods used in the field.
- Specific skills: focusing on skills like vocabulary, grammar, maths or exam technique.
- Others: hot topics, fact boxes, worked examples, tip boxes etc.

The tips in '**Editing pedagogical features**' can be applied to editing boxes. Also keep an eye out for details like whether the feature is numbered, whether each box has a subtitle ('In depth: The oil industry' compared to just 'In depth') and whether questions are included, and ensure these points are consistent. Check how the feature will be presented on the page; for example if the feature will be placed in the margin you may need to reduce the word count.

Key terms and glossaries

Textbooks use many terms that will be new to students. These are often defined in a glossary and/or key terms boxes. Both features include a term and definition and it is customary to bold the term within the main text, so the reader knows it will be defined. Key terms boxes are usually placed in the margin near where the term is first used; they are handy as they save searching for the definition in the glossary at the end of the book. However, they are not feasible in all text designs and tend to be used more for younger readers, or for more complex topics. Ebooks will often allow for a pop-up definition when you hover or click on the term.

For key terms boxes and glossaries, check:

- the term is boldened according to the brief (often the first occurrence of the term in each chapter, but alternatively the first in the book, or every occurrence)
- the term is the same in the main text and in the glossary (for example if 'economic profit' is bold but the definition is for 'profit' a student might not find the definition in an alphabetical glossary)
- the terms in key terms boxes are ordered as required in the brief (for example alphabetical or in the same order as the words appear in the text)
- definitions are clear and concise
- the term is not repeated in the definition (occasionally this is acceptable, but avoid examples like 'balanced force: when two forces are balanced')
- terms are explained within the main text as well (if this is the publisher's preference)
- the definition doesn't contradict any of the main text (the wording may be different but should convey the same meaning)
- the definition is consistent with the specification's use of the term (if relevant)
- the definition is broad enough to cover all uses of the term within the book.

Start-of-chapter features

Textbooks, as with other types of books, usually include an introduction in each chapter. The introduction might be a very brief description of what the chapter will cover or it could be lengthier, setting the scene for what will be covered, introducing various key terms or theories and setting up the debates in the topic.

Some authors start the introduction with an example, a brief story (vignette) or a thought-provoking photo, to engage the reader in the topic and prompt them to start thinking about some of the key questions that will be discussed in the chapter. Whichever approach is taken in the introductions, make sure they are consistent between chapters and reflect the content of the chapter.

It is very common to include learning objectives at the start of a textbook chapter. These are brief statements of what the student can expect to be able to do once they have studied the chapter. There is usually an introductory sentence like 'After studying this chapter, you will be able to:' followed by bullet points where each item starts with a verb like apply, analyse, remember, evaluate, compare, define, describe or calculate. Alternatively the introductory sentence might include the verb ('you will be able to describe how:') and each item will be a factual statement.

Learning objectives might closely match those in a specification. If the author creates their own, ensure the objectives:

- are kept to a manageable number
- match the chapter content
- are ordered in a logical way (often the same order as the topics are covered in the chapter)
- are worded unambiguously
- use appropriate verbs (be aware that the use of exam board command words or verbs from Bloom's Taxonomy are important in assessment, so don't revise them without consulting the author)
- are achievable based on the chapter's content and the reader's ability.

End-of-chapter features

Many textbooks end with a summary of the chapter contents, either in bullet point form or in paragraphs. This reinforces learning and is useful for revision. But it can be repetitive, especially if similar material is included in the introduction or learning objectives.

Another approach is to draw together the points made in the chapter. This is particularly useful if the chapter has presented various theories, as the author can evaluate and compare the theories and come to a conclusion. It can also be used to identify where future research may go or to link with later chapters in the book.

Some textbooks include a feature to encourage students to evaluate their learning. For example, they might repeat the learning objectives in a table and ask students to select whether they are confident or feel they need more work for each objective.

6 | Pedagogical features

Some textbooks provide a list of further reading and resources (books, journal articles, websites, videos, newspaper articles etc) to encourage students to read deeper into the subject. Keep these to a manageable number to increase the chance of students following the recommendations. It is often helpful to add a brief description to each recommended reading, for example 'A detailed account of theory X by a prominent researcher in the field'.

Chapters often end with activities so students can test their understanding of the chapter, or with a glossary. See the sections on **'Activities'** and **'Key terms and glossaries'**.

As with chapter introductions, make sure conclusions are consistent in style and approach between chapters, and reflect the content of the chapter. If the learning objectives are repeated, check the wording is identical.

7 | Artwork, tables and permissions

Artwork is a catch-all term used to refer to visual illustrations including photos, cartoons, line drawings, diagrams, works of art, graphs, flowcharts, maps etc. Some clients will use terms like 'images' or 'figures' similarly broadly. Tables are usually considered separately.

There are many purposes for artwork and tables including adding colour and interest to the page (this tends to be more important the younger the student is), guiding the reader through a process, helping them to remember a theory, showing links between subjects, explaining a method, showing research results, broadening the students' horizons and so on.

Artwork and tables

Here are some general points to think about when checking artwork and tables:

- Consider whether each artwork or table is useful. Does the graph help students to visualise the relationship between two variables? Is it important enough to justify the space? Would the information be clearer in a different type of graph? Does the flowchart help students see the steps involved, or is it superfluous because there's already a numbered list? Does the photo bring the subject to life or is it purely decorative? (Note that for some textbooks photos are used to add colour and interest to the page and that's fine; for others there has to be a clear purpose to every photo.) Does the table make it easier to compare values than using normal text?
- Check artwork and tables match the text. Does the text describe the pattern shown in the graph (or the results shown in a table) accurately? Does the flowchart accurately depict the process explained

in the text? Do any labels or descriptions in the diagram match the wording used in the text? Does any description of colours or patterns in the text match those in the artwork?
- Check artwork and tables are numbered consecutively in the text. Check whether different types of artwork should be numbered separately (such as maps and figures). It's common to number artwork by chapter, so the third figure in chapter 5 will be 'Figure 5.3'. Tables are usually numbered separately from artwork.
- Check all artwork and tables are mentioned in the text. A possible exception may be purely decorative photos but check with your client.
- Make sure all artwork and tables include a caption, if required by the publisher. Captions should usually be descriptive, but decorative photos might include a thought-provoking question instead. Make sure captions are concise.

Checking tables

Copyediting training and reference books explain the general principles of editing tables. For textbooks the same principles apply; however (in addition to the more general bullet points above), remember that it's important to be extra careful that the layout is clear, that column headings are brief and relevant, and that abbreviations are explained.

In addition consider the age of the reader – a primary school student will be able to take in much less information than an undergraduate, so should not be presented with overly complex or detailed tables.

Checking artwork

In addition to the general points covered above:

- Check there is a suitable number of artworks. Check the number matches the brief (too many can be costly in terms of permissions or paying illustrators and can increase the extent; too few may result in pages of plain text).
- Check there is a roughly even spread between and within chapters. You might aim for an artwork every double-page spread, for example. Of course some chapters might require more artwork or offer more

opportunities for artwork (perhaps a practical compared to theoretical chapter), so do be flexible unless the text design requires a certain number of artworks per page.
- Suggest additional artwork if you feel that it could help explain a concept or would be a more effective way of presenting information (such as presenting a process in a flowchart or changing a bullet point list into a spider diagram).
- Ensure photos and illustrations are suitable for the age of the reader (avoid alcohol, drugs, cigarettes, nudity and sexualised images in most textbooks, but especially those for younger children).
- For international curriculum and ELT textbooks, pay close attention to cultural sensitivities (see the **'Cultural considerations'** section in chapter 3). Some things to look out for include: bare skin (bare hands and forearms may be acceptable), alcohol, drugs, cigarettes, gambling (including dice), certain animals (such as pigs and dogs), weapons, war and depictions of intimate relationships (for example kissing).
- Check for diversity and stereotyping (see the **'Culture, diversity and inclusion'** section in chapter 3 for details).
- Look at all parts of photos carefully. There may be issues with people or objects in the background that aren't obvious at first glance.
- Check for safety in photos or diagrams in textbooks for scientific subjects and some technical qualifications (use of safety googles, gloves, safety helmets etc).

Artwork briefs and logs

Editors are often asked to compile an artwork brief and log. These are important documents for the publisher because they ensure that all the significant details about the artwork are provided in a concise and logical way, allowing them to find or commission artworks, ensure permission has been granted and be confident that the artworks are inserted into the correct places in the book.

The artwork log is a spreadsheet containing important details for each artwork, usually including: the artwork reference (for example 'Figure 4.5'), the chapter/section number where the artwork appears, the artwork type (photo/figure etc), a description of what is wanted (or a link to the actual artwork if this is known, such as a hyperlink to a stock photo site) and the

7 | Artwork, tables and permissions

artwork size (a quarter page etc). The artwork brief might include similar details but also a detailed brief (and possibly a sketch) for any artwork that needs to be commissioned.

Some things to consider:

- When briefing for photos, commissioned cartoons or redrawn graphs and figures, remember that the picture researcher or illustrator may not be a subject expert and may not have read the surrounding text. Make sure you provide enough detail and your instructions are unambiguous.
- When briefing for photos, while you should provide sufficient detail, be aware that the picture researcher will either search from existing photos (so may not be able to find a photo showing exactly what you have asked for) or arrange a photoshoot (in which case not every

request will be feasible). So be clear in your brief which aspects are essential and which are desirable.
- For commissioned cartoons and line drawings explain your requirements as clearly as possible; these are expensive so the publisher will want to avoid revisions.
- Figures like graphs and flowcharts are often redrawn to improve quality and to convert them to house style. Ask the author to provide a sketch as close as possible to the final version, with clear instructions about any changes.

Permissions

Check who is responsible for securing permissions. There will often be a permissions editor assigned to this task. You may nonetheless be asked to compile a permissions log detailing any artwork, table or piece of text that needs permissions to be cleared.

A detailed explanation of permissions is beyond the scope of this guide. A few pointers include:

- Anything taken from another source may need to have permissions cleared. While there are possible exceptions for 'fair dealing' (or 'fair use' in the US) these are not clearly defined, so tread carefully and seek advice from your client.
- Encourage authors to record where they find text and artwork as soon as possible, to avoid losing track.
- Clients will often have accounts with large picture libraries. Using artwork from these is usually straightforward and often cheaper for the client.
- Just because a picture is online, it doesn't mean the author can use it without clearing permissions.

8 | Multi-component products

Multi-component products are ones where a number of resources are built around the main student textbook. They can add various challenges to editing textbooks, but also offer opportunities for more varied work. Editing just one component can also be a good introduction into editing textbooks, as they may be less complex.

Editing multi-component products

Many textbooks include multiple components in addition to the main student textbook, for example:

- Teacher book: teaching ideas, lesson plans and worksheets.
- Workbook: practice questions for students.
- Revision guide: condensed coverage of the topic for revision, plus practice questions and exam advice.
- Scripts: audio and video.
- Enhanced ebooks: ebook version of the printed textbook with added features like interactive activities, audio and video.
- Online resources for students: quizzes, activities, worked examples, flashcards, audio and video.
- Online resources for teachers: answers, test banks (quizzes they can use with their students), progression trackers, lesson plans, PowerPoint slides, lecture notes, figures from the textbook, schemes of work.

You may be asked to edit just one component, or any number of them, either concurrently or consecutively.

The advice in this guide holds for the main aspects of editing each of these components. Of course, the audience for some components is the teacher rather than the students, but you can adapt the process accordingly. For example, the advice on editing text for students with English as an additional language (see **chapter 3**) also applies to working on text for teachers with English as an additional language. It's also still relevant to consider how much subject expertise (plus how much teaching experience) they are likely to have – teachers sometimes teach outside their main subject area, so for some teacher resources you'll need to be careful about how much prior knowledge to assume.

For online resources there may be differences in how you complete the edit. For example, online quizzes might be written into a template. The CIEP course '**Editing Digital Content**' provides excellent advice and practice. Editing in PowerPoint may be unfamiliar and tracked changes are not possible; ask your client if they have a preferred method, like using comments or providing a list of changes in a separate Word or Excel document.

Checking consistency between components is usually important. A few resources might be related to the topic overall and will still be relevant even if some content in the main textbook changes. But most resources are closely linked to the main textbook so consistency is essential. For example, if a subsection in the textbook is rewritten then a practice question on this content at the end of the chapter needs to be rewritten, which means the answer in the teacher book needs to be rewritten, as well as the bullet point summarising this subsection on the separate scheme of work, plus the interactive quiz that includes two questions on this subsection. It is very easy to make changes in one place and forget what they impact elsewhere, and this is something to keep a close eye on when editing multiple components. It can be useful to keep a log of changes and their possible knock-on effects.

Checking that components are consistent is, in the first place, much like checking consistency between chapters or checking the content matches the specification, but it is an added step for multi-component projects that should not be neglected. It could require anything from large-scale checks (does the content match?) to stylistic checks (is 'Scheme of Work' consistently capitalised?). If you are only working on the 'additional' components (and not the main textbook) you may need to factor some time into your quote for familiarising yourself with the main textbook.

Scheduling and keeping track of versions can be challenging. Often the schedules for the main textbook and additional components will be staggered, but any delays in the main textbook will have a knock-on effect on the additional components. If the schedules are only staggered by a few weeks, then the additional components will be written based on the main textbook author's first draft. This means that changes to the main textbook during development require revisions to the additional components. It's essential to keep track of which version of the main textbook chapter the additional component is matched to.

Related work in educational publishing

The first part of this chapter discussed what is, in some ways, an extension to traditional textbook editing, although many would now see working on these types of material as a standard part of textbook editing.

There are numerous other tasks involved in textbook and educational publishing, and you could apply your understanding of the market to a variety of other roles. Examples of roles you could do alongside textbook editing (perhaps even for the same project, in some cases) are:

- picture research
- organising and attending photoshoots
- clearing permissions
- fact-checking
- organising and analysing peer reviews
- equality, diversity and inclusion reviews.

Other related roles include:

- writing (for example writing activities, adapting materials for PowerPoint slides)
- project management
- market research
- commissioning.

9 | Resources

CIEP fact sheets and guides

CIEP information team (2020). Working with packagers. CIEP fact sheet. **ciep.uk/resources/factsheets/#WWP**

CIEP information team (2022). Editorial judgement. CIEP fact sheet. **ciep.uk/resources/factsheets/#EJ**

Thompson, M (2020). *Pricing a Project: How to prepare a professional quotation.* 2nd edition. CIEP guide. **ciep.uk/resources/guides/#PP**

Courses

The CIEP. Editing Digital Content. CIEP course. **ciep.uk/training/choose-a-course/editing-digital-content**

The CIEP. Word for Practical Editing. CIEP course. **ciep.uk/training/choose-a-course/word-practical-editing**

The Publishing Training Centre. Rewriting and Substantive Editing (Non-Fiction). PTC course. **publishingtrainingcentre.co.uk/courses/virtual-classroom-courses/editorial-2/rewriting-and-substantive-editing-non-fiction**

Industry websites, blogs and podcasts

Bloom's Taxonomy is explored on many websites including: **britannica.com/topic/Blooms-taxonomy** and **cft.vanderbilt.edu/guides-sub-pages/blooms-taxonomy**

IATEFL (ELT): **iatefl.org** (including Materials Writing Special Interest Group: **mawsig.iatefl.org**)

Tes (school education): **tes.com**

TESOL (ELT): **tesol.org** (including Materials Writers Interest Section in **tesol.org/connect/communities-of-practice**)

Times Higher Education: **timeshighereducation.com**

Wonkhe (higher education): **wonkhe.com**

Culture, diversity and inclusion

American Psychological Association's inclusive language guidelines: **apa.org/about/apa/equity-diversity-inclusion/language-guidelines**

The Conscious Style Guide: **consciousstyleguide.com**

Resources from Crystal Shelley: **rabbitwitharedpen.com/conscious-language**

UNESCO (2017) Making textbook content inclusive: A focus on religion, gender, and culture: **unesdoc.unesco.org/ark:/48223/pf0000247337.locale=fr**

Plain English and writing style

Cutts, M (2020). *Oxford Guide to Plain English*. New York: Oxford University Press.

Finley, L, Ripper, L and Carr, S (2019). *Editing into Plain English*. CIEP guide. **ciep.uk/resources/guides/#EPL**

Pinker, S (2014). *The Sense of Style: The Thinking Person's Guide to Writing in the 21st Century*. New York: Penguin.

About the author

Hetty Marx is a textbook development editor and Advanced Professional Member of the CIEP. She has worked in textbook publishing since 2004, including as a development editor at Pearson and a commissioning editor at Cambridge University Press. She started her freelance development editing business in 2016 and has worked on school and university textbooks for a range of publishers, specialising in social sciences.

hettymarx.com

Acknowledgements

A big thank you to Harriet Power, the CIEP information team and the reviewers for their insightful comments and suggestions on earlier drafts of this guide. Special thanks to Rudi, Matilda and Helena for their encouragement and helpful ideas.

www.ingramcontent.com/pod-product-compliance
Lightning Source LLC
Chambersburg PA
CBHW050157130526
44590CB00044B/3383